Beautiful Pain

Beautiful Pain

COLBY DRIGGERS

WIPF & STOCK · Eugene, Oregon

BEAUTIFUL PAIN

Copyright © 2020 Colby Driggers. All rights reserved. Except for brief quotations in critical publications or reviews, no part of this book may be reproduced in any manner without prior written permission from the publisher. Write: Permissions, Wipf and Stock Publishers, 199 W. 8th Ave., Suite 3, Eugene, OR 97401.

Wipf & Stock
An Imprint of Wipf and Stock Publishers
199 W. 8th Ave., Suite 3
Eugene, OR 97401

www.wipfandstock.com

PAPERBACK ISBN: 978-1-7252-7818-9
HARDCOVER ISBN: 978-1-7252-7819-6
EBOOK ISBN: 978-1-7252-7820-2

Manufactured in the U.S.A.   07/09/20

Contents

Beautiful Pain of Adoption

Beautiful Pain | 3
A Mother's Bravery | 4
Lost and Found | 5
Selfless Subtraction | 7
The Third Love | 8
Sovereignty | 10
Blue Eyes | 11
Beautiful Ordeal | 12
Lost Friend | 14
Entertaining Protector | 16

Joy Despite the Difficult

Watch Where It Flies | 19
Quick Change | 19
Hidden Surprise | 19
My Turn Next Time | 20
Uncanny Timing | 20
Wrapped Finger | 20
Old Parenting | 21
Smile At Me | 21
Fluid Surprise | 22
I Need To Workout | 22

Beautiful Pain of Life

Eternal Wish | 25
True Love | 29
The Reason For Pain | 30
Grip of Pain | 32
Eternal Thirst | 33
Cylie | 35
Desire For What I Hate | 37
When My Time Ends | 38
Pursuit of Happiness | 39
Wisely Backwards | 40
The Other Side | 41
Embracing Death | 42
Crosby Q | 43
Blessing of Pain | 45
Desire to Better | 46
Difficult Decision | 47
Death Story | 48
My Lovely Wife | 50
Unending Ignorance | 51
Division | 52
One Makes the Other | 53
Her Silent Pain | 54
The Pain I Cause | 57
Pain Relieved | 58

Beautiful Pain of Adoption

Beautiful Pain

Beautiful pain delivered you to us
Sovereign plan of answered prayer
In Adonai we've learned to trust

Years of unanswered plea feeling unjust
Wailing to God of our despair
To impart that beautiful pain that brought you to us

Glorious day the angel called to discuss
Fulfillment of that dream we did bear
Showing us in Adonai to learn to trust

We drank in your beautiful face to excess
Upon God's blessing we did stare
Due to that beautiful pain that brought you to us

Taken away brought unimaginable distress
Through pain all hope was relinquished to the preparer
But in Adonai we've learned to trust

Miraculous consent brought forth from dust
As the preparer removes another layer
Of the beautiful pain that delivered you to us
Thank God, In Adonai we've learned to trust

A Mother's Bravery

A barren empty crib longs to be filled
Our minds wonder to what you must endure
A joyous day that's sure to leave you chilled
Tears will tumble while we pass through this war
I admire your bravery and courage
As selfless a mother that's yet been known
With people's questions I'm sure discourage
Explanation yet again as you drone
There's another path you choose for your boy
One that quickly forks in the road from you
When the devil beckons to just destroy
Listen closely to God's whisper break through
You have chosen life for his creation
And he continuously loves you beyond explanation

Lost and Found

November 15, 2019
The light left from me
To experience the unforeseen
My soul within me aches

For 5 hours, my wife and I, did you lay between
Then did your birth mother request to see
You'd be right back we did deem
If only we'd known the stakes

Never to return did it seem
We longed to once more see thee
To hear your voice, to see you gleam
You can't be gone, it must be a mistake

How can this be true, it was obscene
It was to be God's plan, we did agree
Unfair!—we shouted- was the gasoline
Upon the fire did it detonate

God's plan felt so perfect as if foreseen
Only trust in God would set us free
From this nightmare we had convene
Faith, humility, and prayer did we uptake

We leaned upon what James did mean
To remain steadfast through the deep, dark sea
In God's plan must we lean
In His sovereignty must we awake

Then a miracle, all part of God's routine
God's brilliance and plan in objective actuality
Like a shot of amphetamine
God's plan was our view, however opaque

Back to us you came through the smokescreen
Our boy came back from being an absentee
Your birth mother did choose what was not foreseen
To reunite you to us and see the daybreak

When the ship seemed to careen
When from the ground was ripped the tree
When we begged God to intervene
When we thought God would never awake

He had a plan so keen
We could never understand the key
He reminded us to remember who was supreme
Who controlled the universe down to every snowflake.

November 15, 2019
A day I wished would never be
Did turn into a nightmarish dream
A day I am thankful for and would never remake.

Selfless Subtraction

Our puzzle is almost to completion
She signed on the dotted line
She has chosen our family for accretion

A present from the best Christmas season
A piece of God's ultimate design
Our puzzle is almost to completion

Tears of happiness are of reason
Your beautiful smile we will get to see shine
Because she has chosen our family for accretion

We get to aid you through all of life's mission
Thankful, are we, for your mother's storyline
For our puzzle is almost to completion

You see, son, she loves you more than realization
She wanted the best for you to align
Selflessly, she has chosen our family for accretion

The Lord is good with his creation
And for your mother, we thank the divine
Our puzzle is almost to completion
For your mother chose our family for accretion

The Third Love

Will I be a good father
One that will make your first love proud
She's trusted me with her toddler
Which whom I will protect with my life, I vow

I know you were not my son
You belonged to two before me
Though your life has just begun
God knew you before He planted His first tree

He stitched you together in your first love's womb
And to His heart you'll always beat.
You burst forth into the bright room
Then your first love did you meet.

She loved you as part of her own soul
T'was why in anguish she let you go
For you she had a specific goal
She knew without her, you had to grow

Now the two before have entrusted you to me
I hope I pass the test
I hope to teach you that in Jesus you're free
I hope I put your first love's worries to rest

I get to call you son
But you were named by two before
My love for you pales to no one
But with the first two I share what I adore

You are loved, my boy, surer than a compass points north
By God before your creation
By your first love when you burst forth
And now to me love gives its examination.

To me love's torch is passed
I pray God's guidance leads me to be a good father
And that my love for you is unsurpassed
However, when I fail, know I'm not the potter.

The potter knows all love to no end
He loves you unconditionally
He sculpted you before to me did he lend,
And only in Him will you find true intimacy.

Sovereignty

For years I asked, I pleaded as my soul longed for you
To fill the empty seat in our family
We felt the task was ours to subdue
Waiting as days tick by so patiently

My only request for our newborn
To know the Almighty so completely
His soul to coalesce with the Son and be reborn
The living water to drink so sweetly

Merciful grace is God's answered prayer
Thankful beyond description
Upon our son's face we finally get to stare
The next chapter—God's written this transcription

I want more for my son, for him to be blessed
To not understand a lack of anything
This race he has begun, I pray he's the best
His favor sealed by God's signet ring

God speaks as he pleases and designs so intricately
Reminding me of my first answered plea
What more could I squeeze from God's decree
That hasn't already been fulfilled perfectly, intently

Who is the clay to demand the sculptor's conformity
God's plan is written for his child
From this clay He will beautifully mold his artistry
And upon completion, step back and smile

Blue Eyes

Staring so focused, so fully, the two profound orbs call to me
Mesmerized by the deep blue corridors, they tease with their flirtation
Dragging me, pulling me, like at tenacious tractor beam they plea
Into the depths I leap—diving from the towering cliff without hesitation
The deep royal envelopes with radiant warmth that surrounds me
Pure bliss cascades, jostles, and jolts every nerve fiber with elation

What's it like when those born blind receive sight
To open their eyes and take in the first of light's donation
Delight reigns over me when my eyes are freed to the deep blue so bright
A feeling— a calling— I've never known and until now was in desolation
How did I ever survive, could have ever thrived, without this new insight
Instinctual duty, I must answer the call, of the deep blue of my boy's supplication

Jireh bids me assurance of unknown desires already provided
Shalom escorts me through the dark and distant duration
Rapha holds so close, comforting amidst any trial with which whips has chided
I will proclaim Nissi until my time here meets its final expiration
Seeing love through Jehovah's eyes brings a new vision upon which he has confided
A new meaning to the sacrifice put forth from His son's sacrificial obligation

Beautiful Ordeal

Today, son, you are two months old
Upon our hearts you have a stronghold
You seem to know it well
Because our bidding you do compel

You refuse to finish your food
From your mouth it has spewed
Or else you fall asleep while you eat
And upon your head we must apply a wet sheet

At times it's impossible to wake you
It feels you could sleep through a construction crew
Then you refuse to sleep unless in our arms
But with that smile you sure can charm

You like to wait till diaper change to let it rip
So down the wall it does drip
We know you really mean to comply
But you sure have a devilish look in your eye

To the swing we set you to be able to see
All of the world until you decree
It's time to be held again is your desire
And this is not ours, but your empire

We rock you, we hold you, we sing to you
We give you a bath and your hair we shampoo
All of your bidding we are eager to do
Because if we don't, the crying will ensue

We may be impatient, irritated, and tired
But this is exactly what we have desired
This love we feel is so surreal
We thank God for this beautiful ordeal

Lost Friend

I have an imaginary friend
I've known him since my time began
As if before me he came to this land
My life from the start he did defend

Into imagination we do descend
First I'm Leo and then Batman
He bounds and leaps and does a handstand
Then true love's honor we both defend

He helps me to conquer mayhem.
When I'm alone, fear he does disband
He's with me always throughout dreamland
To the ends of the Earth and to the bitter end

He tells me termination brought his end.
That he met a match he could not withstand
That now for me, he's my biggest fan
To strengthen me like a true Godsend

He tells me tales of how it could have been
We would have run and played for a lifespan
We would have grown and encouraged to accomplish the master plan
We would have been best buds till the bitter end

We have much in common, much to mend
He was ended, I was placed with life to withstand
I was lucky because he paved the way, my life to understand
He set the path that allowed my life to extend

Because of him I was given a chance to contend
God's grace and mercy extended to me gave my life another plan
Thank you, friend, for this wonderland
I get to navigate till life's end

He says I will soon forget him, others to befriend
But he'll be with me always, holding my hand
Through life's battles and contraband
Until life's taillights we see extend

My imaginary friend will meet me again when we both ascend
To Heaven's gates, with Jesus we will stand
In Holy presence I may finally understand
He wasn't imaginary but a brother I called my best friend.

Entertaining Protector

Son, to what are you staring
When my face you look under?
Eyes full of admiration
A smile so glaring
I can't help but wonder
What's earned such elation?

Reveal your mystery
What do you see
When you stare in such duration
Is it a being from history
A valuable trustee
Your guardian for life's tribulation

An angel ready for war
Fending off all evil
Pulling through provocation
To guide where you explore
And all kinds of people
An escort through any altercation

I hope your gaze
Brings you joy
And a life of dedication
A friendly warrior to slay
Spiritual evil to destroy
Until life's conclusion

Joy Despite the Difficult

Watch Where It Flies

My boy produces much dung
With his hands it has flung
All over it goes
All onto his clothes
And it ends up on my tongue

Quick Change

Changing your diaper quickly is always the case
To beat our previous record is the pace
Before the hose
We have to expose
Let's it spray all over my face

Hidden Surprise

Holding you is always worthwhile
When you look at me with that smile
Little did I know
Beneath that glow
You're producing a massive pile

My Turn Next Time

I dare not open them, for my eyes are shut tight
When I hear that desperate cry out at night
I am awake, I admit
But I move not a bit
For it's my wife's turn tonight

Uncanny Timing

You're finally asleep and not an eye you pry
I get to relax, for my feet make me want to die
To sit and unwind
From this ceaseless grind
When immediately you start to cry

Wrapped Finger

When you start to cry it's sometimes a riddle
Both of my thumbs I start to twiddle
With that sly eye
I think I can spy
That you're playing me like a fiddle

Old Parenting

I'm thrilled for you to awaken and your eyes to peep
We'll laugh and play, good times to keep
Then I will recall
My age most of all
And hopefully soon you'll be back to sleep

Smile At Me

You laugh at mom with her silliness
So I try my hand at this foolishness
No matter how my eyes distort
Or how my face does contort
You just stare at me emotionless

Fluid Surprise

We're about to leave for church
And upon my knee you perch
You start to rumble
Your tummy to grumble
And you throw up on my shirt

I Need To Workout

Finally, I set you in your seat
My arms are tired and in defeat
You don't seem to care
Back to my arms you do declare
My grieving muscles are in need of prayer

Beautiful Pain of Life

Eternal Wish

Before my eyes are opened, the soot I smell smoking
Into the depths of my nostrils the smoke swam
As I try to pry my eyes open, upon the smoke I sit here choking
Finally my eyelids do open and my eyes do the obscene exam
Unbelievable is what I'm seeing as I sit among the ashes, knowing I'm in a jam
For I don't know where I am

Then upon me comes a beast, and the deep thump of my heart does increase
Within a brief moment I beckon my feet to scram
Only one step I have taken when the heavy, heaving chains are shaken
To my face I fall—prostrate, shamed, and shackled I have a new problem
The beast closes upon me, his wretched breath smelling like rotting, burning ham
"Anguish" he whispers "is my name and that of which I am."

"Where am I," I groan, "and why am I in this fiery, fog all alone?"
With a grimace the beast, called Anguish, explains that I am the damned.
"You're exactly where you should be, with the forsaken, and I congratulate thee
On turning your back to the one they call 'I Am.'"
I cry, "There must be some mistake, I've always helped others and acknowledged the lamb.
I don't belong in this place that I am."

"Others I always accepted and their harm I halted, intercepted.
A good person, everyone says that I am."
Then the beast that is called Anguish does explain why I must languish
In this place forsaken before time began.
"We all believe in the lamb, but to him, more is required from every man.
Into their soul they must accept the I Am."

"Again, I congratulate you, we're thrilled to accommodate you.
In this place rid of the Son of Man."
I said, "This can't be right, must be a mistake, all the things on Earth I did were great
I never missed a Sunday and through a sea of sermons I swam.
Throughout my life I was always nice and neat and neighborly, I can't be part of the damned.
I am not this person you say that I am."

"These people here were evil," said I, "now for their actions they are in retrieval
Of the eternal punishment placed for the sins of man.
I've always done more than anyone, my accomplishments will not be outdone.
More than all the other people, I gave most to foreign places like Japan.
Not a single person gave more than me to charity, I must have passed the exam.
You don't know who it is that I am."

"If in this forsaken place I must spend forever, then please go on this endeavor
To my family and warn them of the danger without the Lamb.
They've all accomplished many great things, but I'm afraid the same mistake they will bring
Upon themselves with the rejection of the Son of Man.
You must warn them for me—away from this place, the dark, they need to have ran.
Into their soul they must accept the I Am."

"They'll finally get it if they see you, a warning from such a beast must be true.
That they're in desperate danger of eternity without the lamb.
No stubbornness will suffice, for you can entice them to reconsider and think twice
I beg you, please, to help them understand.
My nightmare will only expand if I see my family in this place void of the Son of Man.
Convince them to truly trust in the great I Am."

"Perhaps I neglected the knock, but please tell me time has not run out on their clock.
Anguish is your calling, but I beg—I'll bargain with you to have mercy on my clan.
My soul you have already taken; to the truth you must open their eyes and awaken.
They don't deserve to be trapped in this place where repugnant rot began
You must open their eyes to this ultimate lie, this sham.
I implore you to not have them perish where I am."

"Enough!" says the beast, "your family belongs here with the deceased.
Even if I stood before them brooding and twice the size of an average man
They would still be one of us, appalling, as they neglect the calling
Sent to them by the Son of Man.
If they couldn't hear the knock, they can't hear the siren, shout, or slam.
If they miss the whisper, they miss the great I Am."

Anguish declares, "The condemned attempt to justify why they preserve the blind-folded eye
When the slightest sight would lead to the lamb.
The judge knocks for all, but it is up to the blindfolded to answer the call.
An endless myriad of knocks throughout a lifespan.
One must simply peep through the hole to discover the Son of Man.
But most care not to escape this decrepit place that I am."

The beast snarls in disdain; having to speak of the one who was slain
Seems to enrage Anguish and with pain is overran.
He growls, "The distracted have missed it—Adonai came to admit,
But you turned your back to the blood of the lamb.
I don't want to hear your accolades, they mean nothing, like chasing the wind of a fan.
Without faith, you know nothing of the I Am."

Understanding washes over me, how could I have acted so arrogantly
To ignore all the whispers of the lamb.
Looking back, I can hear the knock, but invariably kept the door locked.
If only I acknowledged the one in whom life began.
The beast was right, I had ample opportunity to change my eternal plan.
Now I'm here, forsaken, in this place void of the I Am.

If only I had opened my eyes to truly gaze at those blue skies
Taken off the blindfold to understand
Stopped just a moment to ponder the opportunity I had to squander
To ignore the sacrifice of the Lamb
I could have seen the love gracefully given by the death of the Son of Man.
And I wouldn't be in this place that I am.

My new hope is for my family to avoid this anguish, this agony
That they take off the blindfold and gaze at the Son of Man
That they awaken and avoid eternity here with this barbaric beast forsaken
And in splendor embrace the Lamb
To relish the presence of the one from whom time began
That they see the purpose is the I Am.

True Love

As the gallant warrior loves the blade
Does love extend like a ray of sun
As a smooth river flows into cascade
Is love inevitably overrun
To feel the thrill, a desire to conquer
Commodity obtained through battle won
Love's deep emotion to quickly conjure
Fragile desire with delicate scission
Feelings do succumb to self-indulgence
Only by covenant will love suffice
Unbreakable tether shuns destruction
Unyielding choice attains love's gleaming heights
As my soul is held by the oath of God
Love's a choice and not emotional façade

The Reason For Pain

Why do we undergo unexplainable pain
When all hope is lost and all comfort detained
When we have nothing left but to cry out to I Am
Heart-wrenching pleads to end the river of pain, send the dam

Perhaps the agony is an exquisite disguise
Squeezing from the cocoon emerge beautiful butterflies
As labor begins with screams and ends with tears
Does the bright light shine through the fog of fears.

Through the most excruciating of times is the man made
As the sculpture is chiseled, carved, and weighed
Our malevolent passengers we must endure
To shed their claws, to win this war

We reach the goal when our trials wave the white flag
To reveal what was underneath and remove the gag
Our river of pain has slowed to a creek
The screams of agony now nothing more than a squeak

The reflection brings sight as if by design
When our eyes meet with the potter our objectives align
To look on the past with spectacles brings clarity
Upon which we understand God's charity

To be thankful for our unimaginable pain is illogical
Rejoicing through our tears is paradoxical
It's after the fire when the seedlings most flourish
A new beginning thanks to the ashes that nourish

Who am I to say what fires should be
Upon which battles my action should see
The anointed is to decide my pathway
I am but a pawn, nothing more than the clay

Thankful for every traumatic squeeze that life guarantees
I'll choose my pain over the comfort of ease
Because of strife I learn to rely on I am
The ultimate gift is knowing the outcome of the exam

I am who I am because of the pain that life will install
I am who I am because I know the designer of all
Thankful for God's true blessings of sorrow
Thankful to know the one who has created tomorrow

Grip of Pain

Deep in our flesh do the claws take root
Shame of our decisions does our weakness brew
Voices in our mind continually persecute

Our secret under interrogation and still we're mute
To rip the claws would be embracing vulnerability's view
Deep into our flesh do the claws take root

Admittance allows others to solute
Our acceptance of wrongs and a desire to renew
The voices in our mind that continually persecute

Weakness made strong through the one in pursuit
Of our deepest regrets, to cleanse us anew
But deep into our flesh do the claws take root

Exposing the wounds requires faith undisputed
Unexplainable urge to rid this burden's tattoo
And the voices in our mind that continually persecute

Through our weakness his power does impute
In our weakness we are strong because of the one who can subdue
That which is deep in our flesh where the claws take root
And the voices in our mind that continually persecute

Eternal Thirst

A dry wasteland bare of any precipitation
Insatiable yearning for water to satisfy my thirst
Trying to fill the void with any hydration
A futile effort, longing to be reversed

Unexplainable thirst unquenched by water
As if the liquid passes right through
My soul longs for the potter
More than water I must pursue

To sip from the fountain never-ending
Opens eyes to what was previously unknown
Satisfying the urge that was unrelenting
A new ambition that must be grown

How could anyone veil the noise
Without the fill the fountain bestows
Understanding that all else destroys
With the drink, true reality is exposed

I'm addicted from the first touch of the lip
More water from this fountain I must consume
As if life depends on obtaining one more drip
From this fountain that began inside a tomb

I fill my lungs with this desirable hydration
While people warn of the deluge
This water brings my salvation
From the noise it delivers my refuge

Stepping left or right in this chapter or the following
This water beckons to be absorbed
My steps guided to the fountain swallowing,
Breathing down the water forevermore

Cylie

Your greatest gift surprises you with a ploy
As you are beckoned to awake before the dawn
Draining nights awakening to feed your boy
His blue eyes hypnotize your body to trudge on

Every fiber of your being just wants to lie upon
Anything that allows your eyes respite
You find the strength that seems foregone
For your family you awaken with the starlight

You've prayed for this boy long before tonight
Thankful for every tiresome step
Exhaustion, this arduous journey does incite
And with a smile, exhaustion, you do accept

Fatigued and faint would leave most inept
But this battle you've already greeted
Sword wielding, you're ready to intercept
Any threat this battle has secreted

Told to lay down your life need not be repeated
Sacrifice is a familiar foe to which you're bound
For your family you are gladly mistreated
By that foe of exhaustion however profound

We thank you, mom, to us you do astound
Resilience you show does not go unseen
To the mountain tops your praises we resound
How can we ever acknowledge you for everything

Like a beautiful painting in the Sistine
Your love for us is intricately detailed
We love you more than we could ever gleam
And thank you for this mountain that you have scaled

Desire For What I Hate

As my body begs for hydration, I can't resist the invitation
I continue to do that which my soul begs me not
Like a dog is lured to defecation, my body continues self-cannibalization.
Engorging myself on the gluttonous rot, all control I have forgot
Why do I continue to do that which bids me distraught?

Grasping at any straw that can replace the longing my mortal body does embrace
How can I possibly move on from this demon's claws?
I feel such disgrace—this grip I am powerless to displace.
I want nothing more than to withdraw from the suffocating hold of these jaws
Crying out in surrender, to my knees I fall

It's then I hear the intimate voice, the simple calling, asking me to make a choice
Cast off the world and fill the yearn with the Lamb
There is but one choice that can move the soul to delight and rejoice
To hope in the man who was here before time began
He understands the struggle, the call, the way that I am.

He reveals to embrace the flaws within me, to turn and face—cease the flee
The call—the claw—may never go away
But through the sacrifice on the tree, there is triumph for those who open eyes to see
For victory is claimed today through the blood of The Way
And with the sword cleansed with blood, my demons, the Son will slay

When My Time Ends

Forget your tears soon when my time here ends
It is but the beginning of my everlasting expedition
In the presence of eternal glory, my time, I will spend

Mourn not, for where I am, the Earth cannot contend
To perpetual bliss will be my transition
Forget your tears soon when my time here ends

My departure, I'm sure, is difficult to comprehend
But please understand the plan of the great tactician
In the presence of eternal glory, my time, I will spend

Until we meet again, meaningless, is how much success you apprehend
Through submission follow the one with all cognition
And please, forget your tears soon when my time here ends

Be thankful for the time that the Almighty lends
Let not a foothold be given to the opposition
In the presence of eternal glory, my time, I will spend

Grateful for this beautifully complicated world from which I ascend
To everlasting paradise in the next chapter of my glorious mission
So forget your tears soon when my time here ends
For in the presence of eternal glory, my time, I will spend

Pursuit of Happiness

Perpetual pursuit of happiness
'round this carousel I obsess
Next item to possess
Next admirer to impress
Upon this carousel I invest
Meaningless is the success
Of this pursuit of excess
Like the wind we try to coalesce
Our quest proves no progress
Finally to the divine I confess
And realize to have more is to have less
Of my perpetual pursuit of happiness

Wisely Backwards

Backward way of thinking, living for the other side
Ignoring what the heart feels, Earthly desires tossed aside
Blind eye to what seems fulfilling, cravings actively denied
Focused on the less foraged fruit, searching through eyes of a new guide

Prying eyes meticulously waiting, watching my every move
Wondering my objective, my desire, my reassuring refuge
Cast from impermeable circles, the empty eyes disapprove
Swimming upstream, battling against the great deluge

Blinders to direct my target, the finish line my only goal
Obstacles continuously implanted to distract, to fall in a hole
Stumbling with a misstep the luscious candy tempts my control
This confectionery pales in comparison to the fruit which makes me whole

The race demands discipline, beating the body conditions for torment
Eyes remain focused without the slightest lean to descent
Evading illicit desires of the heart, pressing toward a spirit intent
Consistency is key to the cumbersome door marked content

Upon reaching the finish line, completing the rigorous race
We turn the page to chapter one of eternity's grace
Paradise with pleasures incomprehensible is our place
Because He lived for access to the other side; Him we get to embrace

The Other Side

What's it like— the other side
The paradise after you've died
To finally make it through life's ride
Leading to streets of gold
More than eyes can behold
All around, perfection to enfold
But how do we understand perfection
When there is no more infection
Of the pain in this world's injection
Will we get bored of the allure
When the streets of gold offer no more
When there is no more paradise to procure

Zion must hold more than we comprehend
More than our thoughts—our senses can attend
More than our mind's ability to extend
For He reaches outside of time's ability
Knows the ends of mind's fragility
And scoffs at our small mind's capability
Arrogance that we could ever tire
More than we could ever acquire
In a single note from His great choir
All of paradise will bow in His wake
His presence alone will make us quake
When in Zion we finally awake
And from eternity we will desire no break

Embracing Death

The thought makes us tremble
In fear we resemble
A puppy shaking and scared
The ghastly man with the sickle
Reminds us of life so fickle
To be taken; for none are spared

Why such the fright
At the end of our fight
A fate we'll all have shared
If we claim what we know
That the end of the show
Is beginning of a paradise prepared

We should embrace the transition
Of our newfound position
In the place absent of despair
Why lack in confidence
If we truly believe God's providence
That in his presence we will share

Not afraid of the finish line
In the presence of the divine
There will be nothing that can compare
Enjoy the race
But the end embrace
For in paradise we are God's heir

Crosby Q

She sprouted before her time like a hasty flower ambitious for spring
Was during a snow storm the beautiful blossom sprung forth and grew
Too excited was the tiny thing that burst toward the sunlight's beam
Upon this world the open curtains flew
Ready to be escorted into the light like a king
As the flower that drove through the ashes came blossoming Crosby Q

For this day her parents prayed, much anticipating her presence
Five weeks too early did her premature existence ensue
As if a new love to supplement what once was a time of emotional torment
It was not long ago her parent's pain was undue
When they gazed upon their departed daughter, wondering of life's unfair treatment
Never to meet another miracle as such brought Crosby Q

The child they lost brought pain unimaginable, undeniable
Seemingly unfair that life this child would never accrue
With great faith the parents found their God reliable
And another pregnancy God said was undeniable to debut
Trusting yet tentative the parents continued cautiously and pliable
Hopeful that they would ever meet sweet Ms. Crosby Q

A miracle unexplainable when God used a balloon as a microphone
So innocently in the garage the pink balloon flew
Barely noticeable yet loud as a torrent did God speak through a megaphone
Overlooked by most but to the parents a noticeable undertone came through
Was but a minute ago when they didn't want their departed daughter to feel alone
So pink balloons escorted their daughter to Heaven's view
They let them fly unknowing one would return to welcome in Miss Crosby Q

Pain unavoidable, a blackened forest with a single flower bloomed
Pain incomprehensible but through the smoke the beautiful will come to view
Pain never to be forgotten with scars our body is groomed
But exquisite is the flower that pushes through the ashes, tenacity to pursue
With God the beautiful is never encapsulated like the Son entombed
Like the beautiful flower that brought forth lovable Crosby Q

Blessing of Pain

Life delivers its blessing of pain
To all who choose to navigate
Each wave a beating of the cane
In a desire to forfeit it does culminate
An endless barrage to devastate

Pain fills the middle of the blessing
Unlike the relief of hindsight
If only we can stop obsessing
About the immediate pain we must fight
Then maybe we can see the blessing
Of our lengthy battle progressing

The end of the battle will always come
To show clarity in the blessing
If only we can endure to become
Grateful for the time distressing
We could be thankful for our piercing, painful blessing

Desire to Better

I long to be better
To see life through your eyes
To live up to the red letters
To take off this dangerous guise
How do I get off the treadmill
Run with purpose this short race
I wish you would take my free will
Force my steps with your pace
I want to feel your heart
With every fleeting thought
I want to be even a small part
Of your beautifully intricate plot

Difficult Decision

A litany of decisions
Barrage of choices
Which one could be right
To choose which division
To grant our voices
Anxiety does incite

Which way to choose
Which path to follow
Knowing not which is right
Praying for cues
To avoid the hollow
Path which leads to spite

Difficult to discern
The road less traveled
To the left or to the right
Guide my turn
So as not to unravel
To this path give me sight

Death Story

Confined and stale, unable to move
In this box lies my body's rot
Encompassed with my favorite suit
Is all I have with me, my lifelong lot

Where is the rest of my beloved belongings
Stolen from me, someone did loot
If only I could find them now
To them my wrath I would impute

I earned every last penny
Deserve every crumb
Worked myself to the bone
To attain success which I have become

I yell and scream, someone must listen
To this injustice that has been done
There must be an ear to lend my direction
Right this wrong that has begun

My cries fall on deaf ears
Don't they know who I am
I slam my fists upon the door
All of this must be a sham

"Let me out of here!" I scream
With nothing but silence in reply
Seems all hope is lost
This injustice must apply

Finally the darkness sparks a light
And I stand before the gatekeeper
I tell of the cruelty I have survived
And wait for him to review my case deeper

He waits not even a second
Before giving me his ruling
Tells me I've missed the point
Of my life which has been so grueling

I'll take nothing with me
And naked I will return
All earthly possessions
Are no longer my concern

The judge will rule on the heart alone
He cares not for the success you've grown
Downtrodden my head hangs
For in my heart, my possessions were all that I owned

My Lovely Wife

My love, how you excite me
When you look at me with that smile
My appetite grows so hungry
Only gazing upon you a short while
My wife altogether beautiful
From your head to your toe
What I want is indisputable
It's in how you make me grow

Standing there all else matters not
All distractions are forgot
Tunnel vision toward my lot
A path toward my bounty I will plot
As alluring as the day we married
Tantalizing with those eyes
Without thinking my legs do carry
Toward you, my exquisite prize

To touch your beauty, and kiss your charm
Fulfills a yearning, my duty
For to you I would never bring harm
My love, my darling, my beauty
I drink you in and take my fill
Your brilliant body to revere
For this bond, God made, is truly ideal
In you, I delight, my dear

Unending Ignorance

Knowledge and understanding escape me
Like a primate launched into space only to sightsee
I've no understanding of what is around me
I drink information to satiate the quest
To take my fill, knowledge to coalesce
The more I consume, the more I obsess
The sweet nectar of knowledge my mind must possess
But the more I learn, the less I know
I realize nothing of this world in which I grow
So many unknown mysteries are lying below

What invisible enigmas could I reach out and touch
If only I knew where to explore for such
I could grab hold and to awareness would clutch.
Are the riddles even attainable by simple sense
Is the mystery too deep, too dark, immense
Where do I look for secrecy dispensed
Unfathomable supply of questions to appease
How arrogant to claim we have entire expertise
Of any divine intricacies we could possibly seize

Division

Left pulling from the right
Endless battle for my soul
In the middle of an unseen fight
Of which I have no control
Splitting in two, struggling to reunite
To make my heart whole

Striving to shake the dark
No escape in sight
Like blood baits the shark
Do I keep inviting the bite
The path which I try to embark
Weighed by anchor's plight

I want to shake loose
Run toward liberation
Be free of the noose
Strangling my salvation
How is it possible to induce
Separation from this damnation

I haven't the strength—the power
To break chains and run
Dark enemies all around look to devour
In need of the Savior, the Son
Mercy given to overpower
The chains, this unseen battle won

One Makes the Other

There is no beauty without the horrible
No admired without scorned
No tolerable without deplorable
No life without the mourned
Wonderfully awful days we navigate
Enduring one to reach the next
Tree tops to sunken lows we mitigate
The bottoms to reach the coming apex

Living atop the mountain high
Never to see the deep beyond
Warrants attitude we can deny
After night comes the dawn
Wonderfully awful days we navigate
Thankful for the lowest lows
Learning to appreciate
The beautifully painful life woes

Her Silent Pain

The sun sets for my darkest night
An evil gloom not mine to blame
His charisma and smile white
Caught my attention that fateful night
When the picture of my life changed its frame
And began my life's greatest shame

Together that night we fanned love's flame
Laughing and staring in each other's eyes
Interruption came to stall the game
When time to leave it soon became.
One last drink was his guise
I awoke having been his prize

The pain radiated to my thighs
Disoriented and dizzy—confused
How did this happen to me, I surmise
This serpent in a man's disguise
He thought me a doll to be used
Upon me his evil burst forth and oozed

I am the strong, not to be abused
Yet I can't escape evil's grip
I don't deserve to be misused
With shame I felt thoroughly infused
Then evil only turned the page on my script
And when I heard, from consciousness I nearly slipped

Baby boy inside me now gripped
My mind's hold to every thought
Constant reminder of how my life flipped
Why would God add this to my script
Tortuous decision my heart has caught
And none of this I have sought

My heart stretched; my mind distraught
One night's pebble creates such a ripple
I can't seem to end the life here caught
In my ripple of incidents that time has brought
Decisions to make my mind cripple
All due to a night's pebble of evil

I'm not the best for this fetal
Body that lies within my being
A new couple will look at him as their equal
And not see a pebble's ripple
More than evil's night of freeing
A night I can't stop fleeing

Horrible, heinous skies are all I'm seeing
Agony of darkest night engulfs me
My heart and head keep disagreeing
The rest of my life, from this, I'll be fleeing
Night that changed my life's marquee
Night from which I'll never be free

Then I hear the whispering voice decree
This burden—this shame—is not mine to bear
Though I was caught in another's evil spree
I'm not responsible for what was done to me
Silently whispering a pleading prayer,
"Take this pain and my despair"

To which the voice again spoke to my dire affair
I am His adopted child
He understands, and in my anguish he does share
He will take my pain, release my snare
Finally, hope when looking through the immense pile
Of evil all began from a pebble in one night's terrible trial

The Pain I Cause

Could you feel my sins cut deep in your side
Rescuing me from punishment earned
For the undeserving you have died

How did the wounds feel in your hide
Was it the choices of many which so deeply burned
Could you feel my sins cut deep in your side

Like being betrayed by your bride
Yet smiling and giving grace unearned
For the undeserving you have died

With my sin, the thorny crown I have applied
For my decisions I deserve to be spurned
Could you feel my choices cut deep in your side

When you looked upon us how did you decide
Enduring pain, to the cross you would go unconcerned
Because for the undeserving you must have died

Due to your sacrifice you have become my guide
Through the Judge, this blood-stained court adjourned
Because you could feel my sins cut deep in your side
Gracefully, for the undeserving you have died

Pain Relieved

Constantly falling
Another stumble from faith
I can hear God calling
Only to turn my face

Constantly stalling
Knowing where I should be
Ignoring the calling
That God keeps speaking to me

I was doing so good
Years without the mistake
One moment, one stumble,
And shame covers my head like a hood
Welling up in my heart comes the ache

Beaten, downtrodden, and downcast
I feel so full of shame
When the hand pushes through the overcast
I see He never left the side of his claimed

Patiently waiting for me to turn back
See my lighthouse through the fog
Take the hand extending through the black
Accept the pull through the fog

See the grace given
By the hand's extension
Though I fall, I am already forgiven
By Jesus' sacrifice, my soul his apprehension

www.ingramcontent.com/pod-product-compliance
Lightning Source LLC
Chambersburg PA
CBHW060429050426
42449CB00009B/2203